Bloom

Poems by
Mary Lee

*To Seamus, thinking
of you! Mary.*

REjoice
PUBLICATIONS
(an imprint of Matthew James Publishing Ltd)

First published 2016 by
Rejoice Publications (an imprint of Matthew James Publishing Ltd)
Unit 46, Goyt Mill
Marple, Stockport SK6 7HX

ISBN 978-1-910265-36-9

Printed by
4edge [a UK company]

Acknowledgements

It is with deep gratitude I acknowledge the many people who helped and encouraged me in bringing this collection of poetry to print. Their support made it all possible. Gratitude for my wonderful family, especially my parents, James and Bridget Lee, and my brothers and sisters and their spouses. A special warm thanks to the Mercy Congregation, Western Province. Warm thanks to my late friend Brendan O'Reilly, who encouraged me from the beginning to pursue my desire to write.

Heartfelt gratitude to the accomplished poet, Kevin Higgins whose numerous books have been translated into several languages. His facilitative expertise has impacted on the development of my poetry. His unfailing interest and insightful commentary encouraged me to reach ever higher since I joined his workshops. I extend my thanks to all the Thursday group of Skylight Poets who played a significant part in editing many of the poems in *Bloom*.

I am indebted to Daniel Bowman, Jr., poet, novelist, professor. He was the first person to edit many of my poems and later the manuscript for this collection. Some of his generous words of appreciation appear on the cover. Daniel Bowman teaches at Taylor University, Indiana and is Editor-in-Chief of *Relief Journal*. It is an honour to have been recognised by such distinguished writers and poets as Kevin and Daniel.

My profound thanks to Anne Dillon for cover and book design and for her personal interest throughout the various stages of *Bloom*.

Acknowledgements are due to the editors of the following publications where some of the poems, or versions of them, have appeared: *Skylight 47*: Letter from Nairobi; Secateurs; Inventory; *Crannog*: The Colour of Emptiness; *Orbis*: Wine; Tears; *The Furrow*: Your Holiness; In Memory of Her; Veronica; *Spirituality*: Your Holiness; These Are the Facts; Veronica; Simon of Cyrene; Bread; *The Linnet's Wings*: Skellig Michael; Lament for When I Did Not; *Time of Singing*: Haunt; Tinnitus, award winner; Anointing, Editor's Choice; *The Passion Poetry Magazine Competition*: Letter from Nairobi, award winner; *The Galway Review*, Vol. 4: Well, how are things in Heaven? Gazing; *The Poet's Quest for God (anthology*, Eyewear Publishing, UK): Celtic Circle.

For my beloved, late parents,
Bridget and James Lee — their absence a felt part
of daily living.

CONTENTS

1 Lighthouse

Thunderstorm, Ownahincha

All day the rain poured
      on the conservatory roof:
pelted, flogged, drove down,
      drowned out all other sounds,
moved with the wind. The torrent
      gushed, bent every rose
in the garden, stripped the heads:
      petal after petal fell, left
each bush bereft of color, of smell,
      every stem naked.

She Ascends

the hill overlooking
St. Bueno's, follows the footpath
around Mael Maefa. Whins fill
the air with fragrance, easing the upward
strain. Summer greenness against
Snowdon's blue-purple bounds,
clouds drape the coast's face.

A presence, palpable as this
Wales' view slows her stride;
conversations on other mountain
days take her by surprise: *your face
is hidden from you, he said, only you
can reveal what your face, the secret
cells of memory conceal.*

Fear of disclosure tightens
the heart, yet, drawn
to this inner landscape,
she takes tentative steps to disclose;
treads toward the horizon
that stretches deep into us.

Quest

Even when I overlook you
I go on looking for you.
I answer to a name and I

don't know who answers
except when longing, insistent

as the ocean overtaking
the shore, must be submitted
to. This longing swings like

a pendulum – what we love
the most makes us most afraid;

I know my courage when I take
my oars and row my heart home.

Sounds of Sea

wash over me
on Maghery Strand –

crests and troughs,
occasions of surrender:

in the flow of emotion,
the soul stirs,

yields to another's ebb;
whines commingle

with waves of joy;
currents of caution

give way to surges of bounty.
At Maghery Strand

I leave messages on the sands,
dance with Atlantic's songs.

Secure

Deep beneath earth's crust,
fire begot igneous rocks,
housed fossil nests,

millions of years away.
On the universe's surface,
boulder-strewn

shorelines; rocks rounded,
smooth at the water's edge;
irregular and sharp further back,

shelter onlookers, stir
trust, confidence
in tempestuous outbursts.

Sturdy to steady on, scan far out
to sea, listen to the secrecy
of the breeze in their crevices.

Formed in the seabed,
their stubbornness converses
with waters' turbulence.

Solid and silent,
surging and boisterous,
remind us of each other –

pensive, proud;
even and strong in
storms; some to anchor on

when thoughts implode;
others to cling to when
torrents overload.

Not alone anymore in an
eruption; buoyant in this wide,
benevolent ocean.

Spanish Point

I hear him in the ocean's roar,
in the wind's whine at White Strand,
along the cliff walk he held my hand,
spoke of blueness and the white
edges of the foam. The light
on the dark strand before the sea came in.
Sand dotted with smooth pebbles
glistened like ebony from the cliff top.
The pebbles' guttural refrain
with each new wave-wash.
He is still holding my hand. I inhale
the salty sweetness of the air.

Rowanberries

Bright red rowanberries
line the lanes of Autumn,
beads of blood on mountain ash,
like jewellery enhancing evening wear.

Sustenance for birds,
sweet treatment for meats.
I pick them, mix them with windfalls and cordial,
simmer and strain through muslin overnight.
My cheerful liqueur of delight.
I add sugar, boiled
berries become jelly,
blush like a robust Rosé

This time of year
I give thanks for every fruit-bearing tree
            windswept,
            rainswept,
            loveswept,
and wonder what did Diarmuid say to Grainne
on *that* legendary mountain ash.

It is Good

Feet send tentacles
deep into earth,
seek a warm space
to celebrate:

sea salts,
sweetness,
tartness,
star stuff.

Sounds, scents:
mountain eruptions,

fragrance of earth,
smells of sulphur,
perfume of roses.

Membrane at the crown
opens to let in light
from the galaxies
beaming it down behind
eyes where
endless sky opens

behind the throat
into the heart –
energies meet.

Celtic Circle

The Cross stands steadfast,
silent before the winds
of an open firmament; stately
in its weather-beaten stance,
storms blow through its eyes
that refuse to spill secrets.

When horizontal and vertical selves
coalesce within the cross's circle:
passion fires daily duties, elevates
worries, grounds yearnings.

I lean on this sacred tree, invite
it to root and shelter me, let
surrender shake routine, free
me to travel wholeheartedly.

Bloom

Nothing compares to its
whiteness, only Atlantic breakers
are as white but they flash and disappear.
This gleams all day; even in utter darkness,
its soft shimmer is perceptible.
Branches coated with thorns don't deter
the desire to pick one – elegance of five
green calyces holding the luminous.

Silvery veined petals, creased,
translucent in the sun, smaller ones,
even when fully open,
half-hide a sprinkle of ochre.
The circlet of stamens surrounds
the stigma: from their depths
delicious fragrance.

I place five blooms in a vase on the kitchen
table; linger by them, imbibe warm wafts,
as if the air suddenly beamed. Beside
my bed, another bunch, the scent's silent
presence, bringing back an old encounter.
For a moment we unite in the aroma
of rose, a labyrinth of love,
the breathing aura of white Rugosa.

Thirteen Ways of Looking at an Oak Tree

A climbing rose bush decorates
the oak tree's leafiness, pink
effusion against greenness.

II
The oak-tree doesn't need rose-bush
appendage, yet the arrangement blends
with June's flourish.

III
The oak tree's source spreads far, deep,
unseen, until Spring sap pushes roots, moves
pebbles and grass from their supine setting.

IV
Sitting under its canopy, the oak tree's plumage
obstructs Summer blueness.

V
Bare from November till May –
grey-green silhouette.

VI
The oak tree's branches brush earth,
cast shadows and solar panels on gravel.

VII
Winter's unpredictability of searing gusts,
and callous frost do not distress
the oak tree's trunk and robust posture.

VIII
The oak tree's years are unknown until felled;
leaves, pockets for seasons' memories.

IX
Profusion of leaves dance lithely.
Yet, the oak tree's abundance is emptiness.

X
The oak tree holds the sun and moon
on its crown, the weight of silence,
the mystery of breezes.

XI
St. Brigid built her most eminent
convent beside an oak tree.

XII
Over sixteen hundred Irish townlands
have some derivation of 'dair'[1]
Kill Dara (Kildare), Church of the Oak

XIII
Symbol of strength, kingship, endurance,
fecundity, the oak tree is often considered
the King of Trees.

---

[1]The Irish word for oak

Bread

Is the word
the work of one
who spreads the germ
in the ferment of earth?

Does it quiver as it roots
the light, burgeons,
appears fecund in grain?

And how long does it bear
the pain of winnowing
until memory leavens
in the gift of bread?

Ode to Bread

Bread my life
my delight
my right

Bread my fatigue
my mood
my mourning

Bread my duty
my gratitude
my food

Bread my banquet
my style
my staple

Bread my hunger
my honey
my comfort

Bread my crumb
my wonder
my union

Bread my repertoire
my healing
my memory

Bread my table
my wafer
my Maker.

Kitchen Table

for my parents, family and friends

Feast or fast, this kitchen table
spells nourishment, the melody
of presence, time does not obliterate
the voices that resonate;

light shines that no space can
contain; aromas no storm scatters,
affection no sufficiency severs.

Parents are the meal and bene-
factors: tears of forgiveness
scatter themselves; silence soothes
uneasy exchanges.

There's a welcome for all around this table,
patience is prized, islands of stability
within the high seas of variability;

the colours of words cover sobs; surprises
soften faces, hurt's rhythms commingle
with candlelight, morning finds a window;
quiet miracles seek no attention.

Haunt

Blue-black smoke like incense
emanates from every tavern
on Mediterranean's edge.

Bone marrow scent:
goats and chickens
sizzle and char;

juicy smokiness. Full moon
spills over sleeping sea.
Satisfied diners.

Fragrances
prolong the spell
of Luotro's midnight hour.

Later, eyes under
drooping lids smart
from smouldering skeletons.

Weary migrant waiters,
cooks, boatmen:
their faces haunt.

Come for a Stroll with Me

Come for a stroll with me.
If I go ahead of you, you know why;
since surgery, you insist
I lead the way on our cliff walk.
Prefer to stay by your side
lest you trip on tufts of grass,
but you persist.

A man saving hay asks:
why doesn't she wait?
you reply: *she's younger,*
hesitate: sometimes I wish
I were her age.

I wait for you – we walk together now;
then sit on a rock and watch the ocean's surge.
You talk about the lighthouse on the horizon,
about light –
within and without
and I want to shout to the lighthouse keeper:
a glimmer is enough.

Reverie

By the beach in Nice,
on Promenade des Anglais,
pebbles cleanse in
Mediterranean blue,
clacking sound
as the sea draws them into
its receding rhythm,
hastens their retreat
and repeats the flurry.
Bathers dip feet
and features in brine
beneath an azure sky;
soak all day
in Riviera reverie.

As dusk dulls sun,
swimmers move
with ebbing waves;
bid farewell to sand,
shore, foam as if they
sense a tinge of emptiness
that nature's pristine
span goes on without us
year after year,
and we disappear.

Skellig Michael

Was the building of this monastery,
the hand chiseling of each stair,
a mortification of the body?

Was it joy to carve two thousand
three hundred steps from sandstone to reach
the pinnacle of the Skellig?

Did the forced quarantine by Atlantic's
turbulent exposure impose indefinite isolation,
bravery, silent endurance?

And was it soul-stirring to witness
the power of ocean surge,
the unyielding persistence of Skellig rock?

Did the monotony of circling, wailing
sea birds dull the senses, quell desire
to raise the heart in prayer?

And was the Divine Word in every soaring
bird, every fledgling flutter?

2 Kinship with the Invisible

Tinnitus

I sit for centring prayer
at Mullaghmore Conference Centre:
...no speech, no word, no voice is heard...[1]
an hour's contemplation.

As soon as the psalm is read,
wind resonates on the window panes,
punctuates the room's tranquility
while the tinnitus whistles in my ears.

The leader encourages:
everything in the human condition
is to be given a welcome during this hour.
I greet my round-the-clock tinnitus
with reserve.
It crescendos while other meanderings
compete for attention – so many
vie for my surrender.

...no speech, no word, no voice is heard...

my *welcome* guarded,
I long for its mellowing in my core.

---

[1] Psalm 19

Wine

A bottle of wine from one of the golden years of the eighties,
perhaps the greatest for ripe vintages Bordeaux
has ever known, he told her as he popped the cork
pouring it into the glass, in her eager hands.

He poured with style, until, glass after glass,
the bottle yielded
an evening as intense as the sun ripening
grapes on that distant slope.
Though once they awoke to a chill corner
in hearts crushed
by struggles and silence,
it was sated now by words on ruby lips.

One bottle: contrite encounter,
forthright promise.
Bitter-sweet memories
of the one who poured, and more.

Secateurs

Having pruned
the bare branch
of dogwood, (knobbly
with immature buds)
she watched sap ooze
to the cutting point:

his ship's ropes
uncoiled, tugged, loosed,
dropping the narrow
widening gap between
stone and steel
her and him

with a hiss and a slap.

Letter from Nairobi

A spill of feather-light seeds
from a jacaranda tree
twirls into my lap.

Heart-shaped, skin-soft. I count
twelve, gathered with care,
near the equator: your home

to mine, in this city square,
heart-shaped.

Lament for When I Did Not

abandon others' opinion of me.
Befriend the present with presence.
Cover shells of egoism

with the tireless tide of cleansing.
Drown grains of regret;
appreciate others;

frequent the solace of surrender.
Greet the face of graciousness.
Heave hospitality on every boulder

of opposition. Ignite sparks of desire
in the twilight of yearning.
Journey to the frontiers of fantasy.

Kindle confidence
in nooks of despair and fear.
Listen to the aspen leaves.

Make friends with grief.
Coax shadows to join
the newness of morning.

Quench the thirst for acceptance.
Plunge into crests of compassion.

Minutes to Midnight

A phone-call:
cardiac arrest.
Continents apart, she keeps watch
in the room of her heart.

She hears the cuckoo-clock strike
three – it cuckoos every quarter
holding her responsible
for the passing of time.

Minutes drift into hours, tears
salt entreaty. Sighs of petition
alter the silence. Seven-thirty,
she dozes – a strange dream:

walking by the sea,
a body floating face downward
startles her – bent double, scared
and scarcely able to heave the weight

onto her left hip, she struggles ashore.
Wakes. A nagging pain in her hip-bone.
Night watch over. Day watch begins a long
journey into the heart of her heart.

Longing

At the sight of his eyes' delight
he rushes through a crowded
street. She's unaware until

he lifts her high into December
twilight – blithely as a child
whizzed on to a parent's shoulders.

Feet on pavement,
he enfolds her in his arms, eyes meet,
sparkle as if stars settled on them.

A sequence of kisses sends
secret resonances: the one he
longs for longs for him.

New Year

I am the lengthening days of the North
full of promise and pain:

my turbulent showers purify falsehood;
my coat of snow clothes you in solitude.

I am the quickener of seeds in the dark
that grow into gardens of diversity.

I am the hearth flame that bakes bread
to satisfy your night's hunger.

I am the joy of gurgling waters, when you
hear them you know life's goodness.

I am the singing streams of love – in them
you blossom like Spring flowers.

Simon of Cyrene

Feet trample, horses neigh,
urgent crowd.

Terse Roman soldiers control:
a hefty gloved hand on his shoulder –
he struggles against heavy grip;

The procession pauses.
A wooden beam descends,
he is no volunteer – a conscript.

Arms expand skyward
to steady the load. The procession
advances, he stumbles.

Irritation rises:
Jewish dignity recoils
under the foreign yoke.

The slope steep, his
stooped figure staggers.

Is his soul as dejected
as his bent back?

The sharp beam cuts
as he curses his people's
oppression. He falls –

the curse dies on his lips;
the bleeding farmer in from
the country that Friday is exhausted.

Now he hoists the wooden weight
and treads upwards.

The Colour of Emptiness

Reluctantly
she celebrates the sacrament
of relinquishing.
First, she surrenders her emerald,
then orange, taupe, and red;
last, she lets go of her tan.
She watches her final leaf
glide to the ground
in silence.

Empty.
Silent.
Bare.

Translucent against the sky,
she begins her vigil of trust:
wonders how to shelter,
with so much surrendered?

She observes every sunrise and sunset
with longing. They bestow silhouettes:
keep desire alive, help her realise
that her exposure and emptiness,
her readiness to receive
offer a new kind of splendour.

Every dawn she celebrates
the sacrament of waiting.

These Are the Facts

The speed and flash of image,
bark of the sound-bite.

The cosmetics of PR and Hello
celebrities gratify.

Technologies dominate desk, pocket,
platform, offer global connection.
Silence is threatened:

the heart's stillness,
as old as time,
behind face and voice;

home of memory,
identity,
spirit.

It hides beneath thoughts and actions,
embraces nights, days, names.

The sanctuary that alters experience
gathers vanished years
wakens kinship with the invisible.

James Lee

Tempered by loss
every good-bye
an ache in the heart.

Beneath his sadness, unyielding persistence:
never cringed even in his painful dying days;
embraced the unknown with reservation.

Confraternities, meitheal[2] gatherings,
visits to cousins and in-laws, his favourite
soundings. Walked miles in the night

to fairs in Headford and Claremorris;
brought home meat and Butter Scotch sweets
when a deal was done. Until dusk in the fields.

He loved to read on winter evenings; heard next
day's lessons. Wept when neighbours
took the boat to England in the dreary fifties;

crushed when disability visited his youngest.
Needles of light would penetrate where grief
solidified and hope drew anxious breaths.

---

[2] Team of workers

Veronica

You move towards him
through the crowd.
Sweat and blood stream
down his face and back.

Your eyes meet.
Your heart rends.
You hand him a towel.

Such a graceful gesture.
It doesn't happen this way
for us. Wish we could carry
his face home on a scarf, veil or towel.

Or, is each of us scarf, veil, towel?
Can we be ourselves
and another?

Is His face being shaped into
our scope for surrender?
Resistance?

And does He look out at us
from a multitude of others
that attract and sustain;
and from faces we would rather
disown, ignore?

In Memory of Her

Though rumours abound about his
threat to the authorities,
you risk the ridicule of observers,
cloaked in shallow
respectability, who murmur
about the poor, disapprove

the wanton excess of expensive oil.
You break through the patriarchal
party; express extravagant empathy:
anoint his feet with Spikenard –
so pungent, it fills the house with fragrance
and it costs a year's wages.

The overpowering musk of your love
links scent and feeling
as he goes to his death,
body marked now with its heavy
headiness for burial.

He calls your action *beautiful,*
As momentous, worthy of remembrance
as the Feet Washing and the Last Supper:
Wherever in the world this Good News
is proclaimed, what she has done will be told
in remembrance of her..
Tenderness
is Eucharistic.

Bernadette

How far back can you remember?
Is music therapy the key to reveal your journey
back, back where?

To the recesses of memory whenever
loneliness gathers, remembers all the good-byes,
moving to three group homes?

Does it unlock the five-year-old's grief,
to give her the best opportunity, they said,
urging residential support?

Giving the best opportunity can cause
unintended violence. You miss the song of the warbler,
strolling by the lake, Mrs. Brennan hanging the laundry,

the west wind in the sycamore branches; your native home:
your permanent sadness, your permanent joy. I know it when
you and I walk hand in hand around the garden, in the fields.

Anointing

Three days before he dies,
she sees him look at his hands
and waits for her to comment
on their diminished size.
She turns away,
tucks in his sheets.

Every day that final week
She shaves his worn face, shampoos
limp, greying once Auburn hair,
gives him mouth wash,
lifts waxen, fluid-filled feet
to a soft pillow, anoints
his hands and temples
with Lavender oil, sprinkles
some on his pillow.

He joins in when she says
a line from a psalm
before leaving to catch sleep
"Out of the depths I cry to you, O Lord"

They look at each other,
their last long, silent look.

How are Things in Heaven?

Somewhere inside, you beckon
to me to look at the sky, hear your
whisper in falling leaves, imbibe
balm from daybreak's freshness,
nestle in October's arms.

Well, how are things in Heaven
and what are you harvesting?
Has the season of surrender
yielded timeless tentacles to
explore the glorious?

Who are we in each other's drama
and how do you see the story
unfold? Will the moon's shade still
surprise and Autumn mornings glow,
flow into theatres of colour after
nights of sorrow?

You're Wondering if I'm Lonely

after Adrienne Rich

My mother ails
daily before my eyes,
reminding that everyone

precious to me will one day die
and I will.
Not ready to die
I begin the purgatory of letting go.

Autumn offers solace
but some mornings the leaves
look like the wind has dimmed
their flourish.

A call to release
false assumptions
and all I think important?
Allow love only
to sculpt me?

The leaves will die and green again —
in relinquishing
they harvest.
These two, colour landscapes every year.
I try to rest into this mystery.

3 Sanctuary

Seen

You recall the sound of stones
cracking on the road. Screams
carry further than the stones,
shame you before all who stare, cold:

A woman caught in adultery
who breaks the moral code, the law
of Moses, human trafficking.

You stand beneath city lights; strut in the
brothel, ready for anything, afraid of everything.
They do not sense the tide of your
tears, nor how vulnerable you feel.

You tremble in the shadows of the night, gasp
for breath to steady your thumping chest;
your muscles tense, sweat prickles
through your clothes; fear of stones ever since.

There's One who sees, knows.
Hearts melt beneath His gaze.
Claims you ever precious.

Your accusers gather round,
finger stones. His silence
does not condemn – it hangs

in the still, warm evening, compels eyes
inward: let him without sin throw
the first.

Fingers loosen one by one; stones drop,
eyes askance, His, light as he bends to write
and dispels the shame that frightens
all condemned by righteousness

Her Approach

for Bridie Lee

Her approach
allowing grace to find a home.

Let the unseen
map her path,
guide and carry her;

sensed its mystery
in times of abundance
and loss, in byre, birth and bond.

Walked the fields at Spring's return,
welcomed signs of new life
in animal, tree and sod.

Days begun and ended
in prayer; months made
memorable by ritual and symbol:
Candlemas
Lenten Fast
Sacred Heart Lamp
Good Friday Stations
Easter Eggs
Harvest Blessings
Holy Water
The May Altar
November Visits
Petitions at the Christmas Crib.

She baked caiscín[1] cakes every day,
brought meals to the fields during hay
saving on Point's Lough Corrib shore,
replenished baskets for
turf-footing in Oughterard Bog;

in the evenings plated food
prepared with patience,
pride and possibility.

We experienced her resilience
when she surrendered.

---

[1] Wholemeal

Remembered

for Patrick

She stands at the window, waits
for his arrival to the haggard with newly
shorn-wool, hay, hoggets. Beckons him
to break freshly-baked bread, drink strong
tea, linger over farm talk: cows, crops, soil
for seed potatoes; asks about the stone wall
he's crafting, machines for repair, animals
for sale at Headford mart the next day.

Years since she filled this window,
her image still vivid where she sat at table,
her welcome palpable. He tastes relished
bread. Words heard in those moments
burn.

Wait

Your story, lost in layers of fear and
denial that such a one as you,
a woman, could be "apostle to the apostles."

Your spirit battered by seven demons –
demons residing in women in their homes today,
chained by bonds that hold them controlled.

Women in the confines of huts and jails,
afraid to utter 'no' to crack cocaine
that mists over memories
of numerous rapes.

You know how others live your story:
women waiting outside prison walls
for partners inside. Wives, daughters,
sisters who wait for news of their men

taken in the night by militias.
They keep vigil still – love
does that sort of thing. They watch
the lives of loved ones ebb.

Then the long wait for the funeral rites –
the washing and anointing of the body –
the last gesture of affection to stroke and kiss
the face of one's beloved.

You know well, Mary, the desperation
of all who watch as the hearse pulls out
from dank prison walls, into a sombre dawn;
no empty tomb for them.

What is it like for you to return to the vacant
grave where you stand vigil for three days
with nothing left to you but yearning?

Bereft, still weeping, thrust into bliss
at the sound of your name, only He knows how
to proclaim. Is it always Easter morning when
two hearts reunite and love's energy breaks through

the constrictions of our daily crucifixions?
First to know your own rising,
you spill your thrill on Jerusalem's sultry
breeze – no stopping your news, your gait.

Will you tell us, Mary, how to weave your wait
into the torn threads of our transitions, so we
can chase from our tombs singing our resurrection songs?

Tears

well up from who knows where,
lodge in your throat
on their way from the source.

Like a reset button,
they ground your actions
in richer compassion.

Salt streams trickle
your cheeks when you grieve,
conceal needs,
dream new dreams.

They sparkle when your eyes turn
skyward and the sun's rays
beam off them.

Like reflecting lakes,
your tears gather fragments
of the face bending above.

Culture

A conversation.
Fruit.
A bite.
A curse.
Consequences
out of Eden.

Watched over
centuries the way
my story has been told.
Twisted
throughout history:
Temptress.
Sin.
Shame.
Banishment.
Curiosity.
Don't open Pandora's Box.

I yearn to cry out
in the hope you might
perceive even the faintest
whisper of your inheritance:
you are my daughter.
Lineage.
Kin. Pinnacle.

I am your capacity to endure,
labour again and again
to bring forth life:
to re-imagine my story
and yours.

Conjoint

She knows two thousand six hundred and thirteen
people personally – their families
and extended families indirectly.

First, she earns their trust before
asking questions that search;
feels empathy for arenas they enter,
bathes wounds that wait for balm;

is their wing of strength when even
the sunrise seems uncertain, experiences
taste bitter and days turn
to cinders and dust.

Wilderness storms blind just
as prospects beckon; nonetheless,
they know best what they deserve
when invited to explore rainbow possibilities.

When the dark drapes their dreams
she weaves clothes of comfort, waits for sobs
to recede; assists them reframe dismays,
list and dissect setbacks, see bridges to be
crossed towards thresholds.

Forgive and forget doesn't work. She asks them
to remember and forgive: name claim, tame,
aim the scars that lurk and limit change.
She stays close when they shirk
the composure of self-compassion.

As readiness peaks, tomorrow replaces
yesterday's wasteland.
Faces mirror the sunlight.

Snapshot

Your exquisite smile
transforms your face.
Your eyes: beady blue beacons
blend with it
to disguise a world
only I know.

Ego

Multiple.
False.
Defensive.

Years shape it;
more than a few
transform its wounds.

New growth throbs
with pruning;

sun's rays
sooth the sores of severance.

New life pulsates,
pushes hidden boundaries,
spills over the hills of grief,
like the blush of a new day.

Insect

The small, round door half-
closes behind her. The knife's
tip about to prick the pulp
she makes her home.

This black burrower
halts the chore in hand: four pounds
weight to be peeled, cored and finely
chopped for spicy apple chutney.

The insect wriggles in its encasement.
I, too, am enclosed by limits
of the unknown and the trap
door of my imaginings.

Gateways

These are people who display ordinary heroism,
fashion their world from fragments,
have faith to live an enchanting illusion,
advance the elevation of others,
assure us everything will be alright,
look for gemstones in the gravel of life,
trust that they inhabit a magnificent memoir.
Imagine something that doesn't exist,
fall in love with those who receive their imaginings,
have courage to confront the things that tear apart,
say good bye.

Practice austerity as gateways to freedom,
illuminate the dark with compassion,
cope with losing everything,
have indomitable cheerfulness in the face of their mortality.

Presence

In all my nights and days
during all our twenty-seven years.

You walked the road with me,
stood by me, untiring.

Listened to my wails,
answered my calls.

Stretched out your hands,
shared your wisdom shyly.

My sanctuary, my solace,
deep well of crystal water.

Gazing

What is the fire you draw to
when you clutch each other
between the sheets?   Paula Meehan

Is it the fire in your eyes
that lights your face?
Or your gaze
inviting disclosure?

Or the lines on your forehead:
furrowed by loss
around your eyes,
on your cheeks,
and chin?
Their origin triggers my imagining.

Or the lines on your neck,
once round and full,
thinned by diuretics and exercise?
I trace my finger
in their recesses.
And linger.

A Loss Recalled

Tears well up like the swelling tide
breaking on the shore –
swell, heave, recede.

Body trembling –
you wait for it to subside –
you enfold me, don't say a word.

Years later there's the residue
of this deluge, unleashed
by love only.

I need you to take my grief,
receive me again
and rock me to sleep.

Your Holiness

Please tell them
to create rituals
that take us from
our winter of exile:

celebrate Presence
honour the mystical
reach into the
soil of memory

to root transience
rekindle latent yearnings
liberate us from the famines
of negativity

the blight of abuse
oppression
exclusion

give shelter
when experience is
brittle, broken.

Nurture vistas of possibility
for grains of wheat to fall,
blossom into harvests
of awareness.

Commemorate His
poised passion.

Anniversary

Silent.
Sharp.
Ten years.

When I think of you
time melts to
fill my emptiness:

tender phrases from
a thousand letters;
some days I see you
everywhere —

in the stately oak
hiding clouds
over our garden seat;

in the dew on the mowed lawn
that transforms a new bed of buttercups
into beady sequins.

Yellow, your favourite colour
reminder of the sun that never sets —
of dawn, harbinger of every day.

Like this one —
you, the light
through my window.

Inventory

I take none of your
mementos when we say
good-bye except your
scent:

the smell of your
breath the day you
fastened roses in
my hair;

the nights you lit fires
on the hearth, your breath,
energetic as the flame —
smell you every time I
bend to light the room from
embers of remembrance.

Distilled in secret cells,
your scent infuses comfort,
compels my spine to trickle
furiously.

Every time we say
good-bye, I smell the surge
of your extravagant love,
my suitcase is light.

Float

Heads bob
in this blue moment.
White sails glide like
swans on crystal currents.

A child skips on easy ebb
tide, another gathers
shells for her mother and
brother.

A couple hold hands,
seize the vacant
seat, cuddle and chuckle;
then move to the surf's

edge, entwine as if a single
person with two hands
and three legs,
Chagall's couple in *Paradise*.

On Silver Strand's canvas,
they float over flimsy clouds.
Warmed by their rapture, I
hurry home in this May moment.

Watch

She sits on Garretstown strand;
watches the tide come in
and waits for it to ebb again.

She sees twenty-one holidays
washed up on the sand like pebbles
drowsing in the August light
after the sea's cleansing.

She smells the fragrances
of love-nests etched
in the rooms of memory:
lingers where wounds were soothed;
she tastes intimacies,
abides in the ache of belonging.

Notes

Bloom p. 12: This poem has taken its inspiration from Peter Jankowsky's memoir, *Myself, Passing By: A Memoir in Moments*, 2001.

Simon of Cyrene, p. 32, Simon of Cyrene was enlisted to carry Jesus's cross, Mark 15: 21.

In Memory of Her, p. 38, refers to Jesus's anointing at Bethany, Matthew 26: 6 – 13; John 12: 1 – 8. The Biblical quote from The Jerusalem Bible.

Seen, p. 46, refers to the adulterous woman as described John 8: 1 – 11.

Wait, p. 51, refers to Jesus's appearance to Mary Magdalene, John: 20: 1- 18. Pope Francis has raised the liturgical celebration of the memorial of St. Mary Magdalene to the status of a feast, (dated 3rd June, 2016); the same rank given to the liturgical celebration of the Apostles. She has the honor of being the first witness of the Lord's resurrection.